Little People, BIG DREAMS™
MICHELLE OBAMA

Written by
Maria Isabel Sánchez Vegara

Illustrated by
Mia Saine

Frances Lincoln
Children's Books

On the upper floor of a humble house on the south side of Chicago, a little girl called Michelle was growing up. Every night, she put her stuffed friends to bed, telling them the same thing her parents told her: "Study hard and be great!"

Her school was down the street, but she dreamt of studying at the best universities—something her parents never had the chance to do. For Michelle, education was about becoming the best person she could be. Someone like…her dad!

When she got older, Michelle took a long trip every day to attend a high school for top achievers on the other side of the city. There, all the students looked different, but were all very much alike: they shared a passion for learning.

Princeton, one of the most prestigious colleges in the world, was her next goal, but one of her teachers didn't think she would be good enough. Far from being discouraged, Michelle was determined to prove her wrong.

Michelle did not just get accepted...she became one of their finest graduates. She even found time to run a care center for minority students like her. She was always there to give good advice and a friendly hug.

From Princeton, she went to Harvard and, from there, right into a fancy office in Chicago. Michelle was now a very busy lawyer. Still, after a long day at work, she loved to join her parents for dinner.

One day, Barack Hussein Obama, a promising law student, came into her office. Michelle became his mentor, but they soon realized they shared a love for family and education, and a strong desire to help those less fortunate.

The day Michelle's father died was one of the saddest ever. His life and love for others inspired Michelle to quit her job and join Public Allies; a non-profit organization that helps young students become leaders.

When Barack decided to run for president of the United States, Michelle stood next to him. She was his teammate, his friend, his wife, and the mother of his two daughters. For them, it was the whole Obama family running!

Barack became the first African American president of
the United States, and Michelle, a First Lady like no other.

The presidential White House, built by enslaved Black people
200 years before, was now a Black family's home.

Growing fruit and vegetables on the lawn, Michelle realized she had found her number one cause: food and fitness. It was not just her daughters' menu she wanted to look after, but the health of young people all over the country.

She encouraged schools, parents and children to play sports and eat nourishing food at home. Michelle traveled the world inspiring governments to build a brighter future for their countries by improving girls' education.

And whatever the future brings for little Michelle, she will keep touching people's hearts and souls. Because she knows that, once you have made your dreams come true, it's your job to help others to do the same.

MICHELLE OBAMA

(Born 1964)

1992

2007

Born on Chicago's south side, Michelle LaVaughn Robinson arrived on
January 17th, 1964, to parents Marian and Fraser. While her father worked
long hours in the city's water-purification plant, Michelle's mother quit her
job as a secretary to be at home with Michelle and her older brother, Craig
Malcolm. Her childhood was a happy one, playing music, and reading.
But the time was not without struggle, as her father Fraser battled multiple
sclerosis. She remembers that he "never stopped laughing, even while
struggling to button his shirt... or get himself across the room to give my
Mom a kiss." This same determination stayed with Michelle as she went
to high school, choosing to use the discrimination around her to fuel her
passion. She studied sociology and African American studies at Princeton

2008

2019

before attending Harvard Law School. Returning to Chicago, she took a job as a junior associate at a law firm where she met Barack Obama, who was hired as the summer associate. They fell in love—united by a desire to change the world for the good of others. After her father died, Michelle felt called to step up her advocacy for others again, connecting to both her city and culture at Public Allies. Barack was elected to the Illinois Senate in 1996, and while Michelle continued her work in law and education, Barack was elected to the U.S. Senate. In 2009 they became history's first African American presidential family, moving to The White House with their daughters Malia and Sasha. Still today, Michelle gives people a voice to speak their dreams—and the means to live them.

Want to find out more about **Michelle Obama?**

Have a read of these great books:

The Extraordinary Life of Michelle Obama by Sheila Kanani

Work It, Girl: *Become a Leader like Michelle Obama* by Caroline Moss

Brimming with creative inspiration, how-to projects, and useful information to enrich your everyday life, Quarto Knows is a favourite destination for those pursuing their interests and passions. Visit our site and dig deeper with our books into your area of interest: Quarto Creates, Quarto Cooks, Quarto Homes, Quarto Lives, Quarto Drives, Quarto Explores, Quarto Gifts, or Quarto Kids.

Text © 2021 Maria Isabel Sánchez Vegara. Illustrations © Mia Saine 2021.

Original concept of the series by Maria Isabel Sánchez Vegara, published by Alba Editorial, s.l.u

Little People Big Dreams and Pequeña&Grande are registered trademarks of Alba Editorial, s.l.u. for books, printed publications, e-books and audiobooks. Produced under licence from Alba Editorial, s.l.u.

First Published in the US in 2021 by Frances Lincoln Children's Books, an imprint of The Quarto Group.

The Old Brewery, 6 Blundell Street, London N7 9BH, United Kingdom.

T 020 7700 6700 **www.QuartoKnows.com**

A catalogue record for this book is available from the British Library.

ISBN 978-0-7112-5942-3

Set in Futura BT.

Published by Katie Cotton • Designed by Sasha Moxon

Edited by Katy Flint • Production by Nikki Ingram

Editorial Assistance from Alex Hithersay • Sensitivity read by Kayla Dunigan

Manufactured In China CC042021

1 3 5 7 9 8 6 4 2

Photographic acknowledgements (pages 28-29, from left to right): 1. Michelle Obama on her wedding day in Chicago, 1992 © Ins News/Shutterstock. 2. Michelle Obama attends New York Historical Society STRAWBERRY FESTIVAL LUNCHEON on June 26, 2007 © MATT CARASELLA/Patrick McMullan via Getty Images. 3. US President elect Barack Obama walks on stage, with his wife Michelle (R) and daughters Malia (2nd R) and Sasha, to address his supports during an election night gathering in Grant Park on November 4, 2008 in Chicago, Illinois © Scott Olson/Getty Images. 4. Former First Lady Michelle Obama attends 'Becoming: An Intimate Conversation with Michelle Obama' at State Farm Arena on May 11, 2019 in Atlanta, Georgia © Paras Griffin/Getty Images.

MIX
Paper from
responsible sources
FSC® C008047

Collect the *Little People*, **BIG DREAMS**™ series:

FRIDA KAHLO 	**COCO CHANEL** 	**MAYA ANGELOU** 	**AMELIA EARHART** 	**AGATHA CHRISTIE** 	**MARIE CURIE** 	**ROSA PARKS**
AUDREY HEPBURN 	**EMMELINE PANKHURST**	**ELLA FITZGERALD** 	**ADA LOVELACE**	**JANE AUSTEN**	**GEORGIA O'KEEFFE**	**HARRIET TUBMAN**
ANNE FRANK 	**MOTHER TERESA**	**JOSEPHINE BAKER**	**L. M. MONTGOMERY**	**JANE GOODALL** 	**SIMONE DE BEAUVOIR**	**MUHAMMAD ALI**
STEPHEN HAWKING	**MARIA MONTESSORI** 	**VIVIENNE WESTWOOD**	**MAHATMA GANDHI**	**DAVID BOWIE**	**WILMA RUDOLPH** 	**DOLLY PARTON**
BRUCE LEE 	**RUDOLF NUREYEV** 	**ZAHA HADID**	**MARY SHELLEY**	**MARTIN LUTHER KING JR.** 	**DAVID ATTENBOROUGH**	**ASTRID LINDGREN**
EVONNE GOOLAGONG 	**BOB DYLAN** 	**ALAN TURING**	**BILLIE JEAN KING** 	**GRETA THUNBERG** 	**JESSE OWENS** 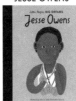	**JEAN-MICHEL BASQUIAT**

ARETHA FRANKLIN

CORAZON AQUINO

PELÉ

ERNEST SHACKLETON

STEVE JOBS

AYRTON SENNA

LOUISE BOURGEOIS

ELTON JOHN

JOHN LENNON

PRINCE

CHARLES DARWIN

CAPTAIN TOM MOORE

HANS CHRISTIAN ANDERSEN

STEVIE WONDER

MEGAN RAPINOE

MARY ANNING

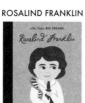

MALALA YOUSAFZAI

ANDY WARHOL

RUPAUL

MICHELLE OBAMA

MINDY KALING

IRIS APFEL

ROSALIND FRANKLIN

ACTIVITY BOOKS

STICKER ACTIVITY BOOK COLORING BOOK LITTLE ME, BIG DREAMS JOURNAL

Discover more about the series at www.littlepeoplebigdreams.com